EMMANUEL JOSEPH

Heavenly Ventures, Integrating Spirituality, Ethics, and Entrepreneurship in Childhood Education

Copyright © 2025 by Emmanuel Joseph

All rights reserved. No part of this publication may be reproduced, stored or transmitted in any form or by any means, electronic, mechanical, photocopying, recording, scanning, or otherwise without written permission from the publisher. It is illegal to copy this book, post it to a website, or distribute it by any other means without permission.

First edition

This book was professionally typeset on Reedsy. Find out more at reedsy.com

Contents

1	Chapter 1: The Dawn of Holistic Education	1
2	Chapter 2: The Power of Mindfulness	3
3	Chapter 3: Ethics in Action	5
4	Chapter 4: Entrepreneurship for Young Minds	7
5	Chapter 5: Spirituality in Education	9
6	Chapter 6: The Role of Community	11
7	Chapter 7: The Joy of Learning	13
8	Chapter 8: Building Resilience	15
9	Chapter 9: The Ethics of Entrepreneurship	17
10	Chapter 10: Creative Expression	19
11	Chapter 11: Global Awareness	21
12	Chapter 12: The Role of Technology	23
13	Chapter 13: Parental Involvement	25
14	Chapter 14: Celebrating Diversity	27
15	Chapter 15: Looking to the Future	29

1

Chapter 1: The Dawn of Holistic Education

In the bustling town of Bellwood, the community gathered to discuss the future of their children's education. Among the crowd, Ms. Thompson, a passionate educator, stood up and shared her vision of holistic education. She believed that children should not only excel academically but also develop spiritually, ethically, and entrepreneurially. Her speech ignited a spark in the hearts of the parents, and they decided to embark on a journey to transform their local school, Bellwood Academy.

Bellwood Academy was unlike any other school. It had a curriculum that intertwined spirituality, ethics, and entrepreneurship. The school's motto, "Educating the Heart and Mind," resonated with everyone. The children were taught the importance of mindfulness through daily meditation sessions. They learned about moral values through stories of great leaders and ethical dilemmas. Entrepreneurship was introduced through fun projects, where students created and managed their own small businesses within the school.

One memorable story from Bellwood Academy was of a young girl named Lucy. Lucy had always been shy and struggled to make friends. However, when she participated in the school's entrepreneurship project, she discovered her passion for baking. With guidance from her teachers, she started a small bakery within the school. Her classmates loved her delicious treats, and soon, Lucy's bakery became the most popular stall at the school fair. This experience not only boosted her confidence but also taught her valuable lessons in business and ethics.

As the school year progressed, the impact of the holistic education model became evident. Children were more empathetic, confident, and creative. Parents noticed positive changes in their children's behavior and attitude towards learning. The success of Bellwood Academy's approach soon spread to neighboring towns, inspiring other schools to adopt similar models.

In conclusion, the dawn of holistic education at Bellwood Academy marked the beginning of a transformative journey. By integrating spirituality, ethics, and entrepreneurship into childhood education, the school created an environment where children could flourish in every aspect of their lives. This chapter sets the stage for the many adventures and lessons that follow in the book.

2

Chapter 2: The Power of Mindfulness

Mindfulness was a cornerstone of Bellwood Academy's curriculum. Every morning, students and teachers gathered in the school's serene meditation garden to practice mindfulness. The garden, with its blooming flowers and chirping birds, provided the perfect setting for reflection and inner peace. The practice of mindfulness helped students develop focus, reduce stress, and cultivate a sense of gratitude.

One day, during a particularly challenging period of exams, a young boy named Sam felt overwhelmed by the pressure. His grades had been slipping, and he was struggling to keep up with his studies. Ms. Thompson noticed Sam's distress and invited him to join her in the meditation garden during lunch breaks. At first, Sam was skeptical, but he decided to give it a try.

Over the next few weeks, Sam's daily mindfulness practice began to show results. He became more focused in class, and his anxiety levels decreased. One afternoon, as he sat in the garden, he had an epiphany. He realized that his self-worth was not determined by his grades but by the person he was becoming. This newfound perspective gave him the strength to persevere and improve his academic performance.

Sam's story inspired other students to embrace mindfulness as well. The school's meditation garden became a sanctuary for many children, a place where they could find solace and clarity. Teachers also noticed a positive change in the classroom atmosphere. Students were more attentive, respectful, and engaged in their learning.

The practice of mindfulness extended beyond the school grounds. Parents were encouraged to practice mindfulness with their children at home. Family meditation sessions became a common evening ritual, strengthening the bond between parents and children. The community of Bellwood began to experience the ripple effects of mindfulness, leading to a more harmonious and compassionate environment.

In conclusion, the power of mindfulness at Bellwood Academy transformed not only the lives of the students but also the entire community. By teaching children to be present and mindful, the school fostered a sense of inner peace and resilience that would benefit them throughout their lives.

3

Chapter 3: Ethics in Action

Ethics education at Bellwood Academy was not confined to textbooks and lectures. Instead, it was brought to life through interactive activities and real-world scenarios. The school believed that children should learn ethical values through experience and reflection, making the lessons more meaningful and impactful.

One of the most popular activities was the "Ethical Adventure Challenge." This weekly event involved a series of tasks that required students to make ethical decisions. For example, one challenge involved a lost wallet scenario. Students had to decide what to do when they found a wallet with money and an ID card. The discussion that followed helped them understand the importance of honesty and integrity.

Another memorable story was of a group of friends who faced a difficult choice during a school trip. They discovered that one of their classmates had stolen a valuable item from a gift shop. The group was torn between loyalty to their friend and doing the right thing. After a heartfelt discussion, they decided to confront their friend and encourage him to return the item and apologize. This experience taught them the value of courage and accountability.

The school also invited guest speakers from various professions to share their experiences with ethical dilemmas. One such speaker was Mr. Garcia, a local business owner known for his fair and transparent practices. He shared stories of challenging situations he had faced and how he made ethical decisions even when it was difficult. His talk left a lasting impression on the students, inspiring them to uphold their values in all aspects of their lives.

To reinforce the lessons learned, Bellwood Academy incorporated reflective journaling into their ethics education. Students were encouraged to write about their experiences, thoughts, and feelings related to ethical situations they encountered. These journals became a valuable tool for self-reflection and personal growth.

In conclusion, ethics in action at Bellwood Academy taught students the importance of making principled decisions. Through interactive activities, real-world scenarios, and reflective journaling, children learned to navigate complex ethical dilemmas with integrity and compassion.

4

Chapter 4: Entrepreneurship for Young Minds

At Bellwood Academy, entrepreneurship was not just about starting businesses; it was about fostering creativity, problem-solving, and resilience. The school believed that entrepreneurial skills could empower children to make a positive impact in their communities and the world.

One of the first entrepreneurial projects at Bellwood Academy was the "Community Garden Initiative." The students were tasked with transforming an unused plot of land into a thriving garden. They had to plan, budget, and execute the project, learning valuable lessons in teamwork, resource management, and sustainability. The garden soon became a source of pride for the school and a symbol of the students' hard work and dedication.

Another inspiring story was of a young boy named Alex, who had a passion for technology. With the guidance of his teachers, Alex started a small coding club at the school. He taught his classmates how to create simple apps and games, sparking an interest in technology among many students. The coding club grew in popularity, and soon, the students were showcasing their projects at local tech fairs. This experience not only honed Alex's entrepreneurial skills but also instilled a sense of community and collaboration among the students.

The school also organized an annual "Young Entrepreneurs Fair," where students could showcase their business ideas and products. One year, a group of students came up with the idea of creating eco-friendly stationery using recycled materials. They researched, designed, and produced a range of products, which were a hit at the fair. The success of their venture taught them the importance of sustainability and innovation in business.

To further support their entrepreneurial journey, Bellwood Academy provided mentorship programs. Local business owners and professionals volunteered to mentor the students, offering valuable insights and guidance. These mentors helped the students navigate challenges, refine their ideas, and build confidence in their abilities.

In conclusion, entrepreneurship for young minds at Bellwood Academy was about more than just business. It was about empowering children to think creatively, solve problems, and make a positive impact. Through hands-on projects, mentorship, and community engagement, the school nurtured a new generation of innovative and compassionate leaders.

5

Chapter 5: Spirituality in Education

Spirituality at Bellwood Academy was not about religion; it was about connecting with one's inner self and finding a sense of purpose and meaning. The school created a nurturing environment where children could explore their spirituality and develop a deeper understanding of themselves and the world around them.

One of the most cherished practices at the school was the "Circle of Gratitude." Every Friday, students and teachers gathered in a circle and shared what they were grateful for. This simple practice fostered a sense of appreciation and positivity, creating a supportive and loving community. One memorable story was of a young girl named Emma, who had recently moved to Bellwood and was feeling homesick. During the Circle of Gratitude, she shared her feelings and was met with overwhelming support and kindness from her classmates. This experience made her feel welcomed and loved, helping her adjust to her new environment.

The school also incorporated mindfulness walks into their spiritual curriculum. Students took regular walks in nature, observing the beauty around them and reflecting on their thoughts and feelings. These walks provided a peaceful and calming experience, allowing children to connect with nature and their inner selves.

Another inspiring story was of a boy named Jake, who struggled with anger and frustration. His teachers introduced him to mindfulness techniques, such as deep breathing and visualization. Over time, Jake learned to manage his emotions and find inner peace. He became a role model for his peers, demonstrating the power of mindfulness and self-awareness.

To deepen their spiritual journey, Bellwood Academy invited guest speakers from various spiritual traditions to share their wisdom. One such speaker was Ms. Patel, a yoga instructor, who taught the students the art of meditation and the importance of living a balanced life. Her sessions became a highlight for the students, who eagerly looked forward to practicing yoga and meditation.

In conclusion, spirituality at Bellwood Academy was about nurturing the inner self and creating a sense of purpose. Through practices like the Circle of Gratitude, mindfulness walks, and guest speakers, the school fostered a supportive and loving community where children could grow spiritually and emotionally.

6

Chapter 6: The Role of Community

The success of Bellwood Academy's holistic education model was not just due to the efforts of the teachers and students. The entire community played a vital role in supporting the school's vision. Parents, local businesses, and community leaders all came together to create a nurturing environment for the children.

One of the most impactful initiatives was the "Community Mentorship Program." Local business owners and professionals volunteered their time to mentor the students, sharing their knowledge and experiences. These mentors provided valuable guidance, helping the children develop practical skills and confidence. One memorable story was of Mr. Johnson, a retired engineer, who mentored a group of students interested in robotics. Under his guidance, the students built a robot that won first place in a regional competition. This achievement boosted their self-esteem and inspired them to pursue careers in STEM fields.

The community also supported the school through various fundraising events. The annual "Bellwood Fair" was a highlight of the year, bringing together families, friends, and neighbors for a day of fun and celebration. The funds raised from the fair were used to enhance the school's facilities and provide scholarships for underprivileged students. The fair was also an opportunity for students to showcase their entrepreneurial projects and creative talents, fostering a sense of pride and accomplishment.

In addition to mentorship and fundraising, the community played a crucial role in promoting the school's values. Local leaders often visited the school to talk about the importance of ethics, spirituality, and entrepreneurship in their lives. These talks reinforced the lessons learned in the classroom and provided real-world examples of the impact of these values.

The sense of community at Bellwood Academy extended beyond the school grounds. Families organized neighborhood clean-up days, community gardens, and other initiatives that promoted social responsibility and environmental stewardship. These activities not only improved the local environment but also strengthened the bond between community members.

In conclusion, the role of the community in Bellwood Academy's success cannot be overstated. Through mentorship, fundraising, and promoting the school's values, the community created a supportive and nurturing environment where children could thrive.

7

Chapter 7: The Joy of Learning

One of the core principles of Bellwood Academy was to instill a love of learning in its students. The school believed that education should be a joyful and engaging experience, not just a means to an end. This philosophy was evident in the school's innovative teaching methods and creative projects.

One of the most popular initiatives was the "Discovery Lab." This was a dedicated space where students could explore their interests and passions through hands-on activities and experiments. The lab was filled with tools and materials for various projects, from science experiments to art installations. Students were encouraged to follow their curiosity and learn through trial and error. One memorable story was of a group of students who built a working model of a volcano using baking soda and vinegar. Their excitement and sense of accomplishment when the volcano erupted was a testament to the joy of learning.

Another innovative project was the "Learning Through Play" program. The school incorporated games and interactive activities into the curriculum to make learning fun and engaging. For example, math lessons were turned into treasure hunts, where students had to solve problems to find hidden treasures around the school. History lessons were transformed into role-playing activities, where students acted out historical events and figures. These creative approaches made learning more enjoyable and helped students retain information better.

The school also organized regular "Learning Adventures," where students went on field trips to explore different aspects of the world around them. These trips included visits to museums, nature reserves, farms, and local businesses. Each adventure was designed to complement the curriculum and provide real-world learning experiences. One unforgettable trip was to a nearby wildlife sanctuary, where students learned about animal conservation and even had the chance to see a rare species of bird up close.

The joy of learning at Bellwood Academy extended beyond the classroom. The school encouraged students to pursue their interests and hobbies through clubs and extracurricular activities. From music and dance to coding and gardening, there was something for everyone. These activities provided opportunities for students to develop new skills, make friends, and discover their passions.

In conclusion, the joy of learning at Bellwood Academy was a driving force behind the school's success. By creating a fun and engaging learning environment, the school nurtured a lifelong love of learning in its students.

8

Chapter 8: Building Resilience

Resilience was a key focus at Bellwood Academy. The school believed that teaching children to be resilient would prepare them to face life's challenges with confidence and determination. Through various programs and activities, the school helped students develop the skills and mindset needed to overcome obstacles and bounce back from setbacks.

One of the most impactful programs was the "Resilience Workshops." These workshops were designed to teach students practical strategies for coping with stress and adversity. They covered topics such as goal setting, time management, and problem-solving. One memorable story was of a student named Sarah, who struggled with public speaking. With the support of her teachers and peers, she participated in the school's Resilience Workshop on overcoming fear. Through practice and encouragement, Sarah gained the confidence to deliver a speech at the school assembly, receiving a standing ovation from her classmates.

Another important initiative was the "Growth Mindset" program. The school promoted the idea that abilities and intelligence could be developed through effort and perseverance. Students were encouraged to embrace challenges, learn from mistakes, and celebrate progress. One inspiring story was of a group of students who participated in a challenging science competition. Despite facing several setbacks, they persevered and eventually won second place. This experience taught them the value of hard work and determination.

To further support resilience, Bellwood Academy incorporated physical activities into the curriculum. The school offered a variety of sports and fitness programs, helping students build physical and mental strength. One popular activity was the "Adventure Club," where students participated in activities such as hiking, rock climbing, and camping. These adventures provided opportunities for students to push their limits, build teamwork, and develop a sense of accomplishment.

The school also emphasized the importance of self-care and well-being. Students were taught mindfulness techniques, such as deep breathing and relaxation exercises, to help them manage stress and stay grounded. The school's wellness program also included nutrition education, encouraging students to make healthy choices and take care of their bodies.

In conclusion, building resilience at Bellwood Academy equipped students with the skills and mindset needed to navigate life's challenges. Through resilience workshops, a growth mindset program, physical activities, and self-care practices, the school prepared children to face adversity with confidence and determination.

9

Chapter 9: The Ethics of Entrepreneurship

Bellwood Academy's approach to entrepreneurship education was grounded in ethical principles. The school believed that teaching children to be ethical entrepreneurs would create a generation of business leaders who prioritized integrity, sustainability, and social responsibility.

One of the most impactful initiatives was the "Social Enterprise Project." Students were tasked with creating business ideas that addressed social or environmental issues. They had to develop a business plan, pitch their ideas to a panel of judges, and implement their projects. One memorable story was of a group of students who started a recycling program at the school. They designed a system for collecting and sorting recyclable materials, raising awareness about environmental conservation. Their project not only reduced waste but also inspired other schools in the area to adopt similar initiatives.

Another important aspect of the ethics of entrepreneurship was the concept of fair trade. The school educated students about the importance of fair labor practices and ethical sourcing of materials. One year, the students organized a "Fair Trade Market," where they sold products made by fair trade artisans. The market was a huge success, and the students learned valuable lessons about global trade and social justice.

To further promote ethical entrepreneurship, the school invited guest speakers from various industries to share their experiences. One such speaker was Ms. Rivera, a successful entrepreneur who built her business on the principles of sustainability and social impact. She shared stories of the challenges and rewards of running an ethical business, inspiring the students to pursue their entrepreneurial dreams with integrity.

The school also incorporated ethical case studies into the curriculum. Students analyzed real-world business scenarios, discussing the ethical dilemmas and making decisions based on their values. These case studies provided valuable insights into the complexities of ethical entrepreneurship and helped students develop critical thinking skills.

In conclusion, the ethics of entrepreneurship at Bellwood Academy created a foundation of integrity, sustainability, and social responsibility. Through social enterprise projects, fair trade education, guest speakers, and ethical case studies, the school nurtured a new generation of ethical entrepreneurs.

10

Chapter 10: Creative Expression

C reative expression was a vital component of Bellwood Academy's holistic education model. The school believed that encouraging creativity and self-expression would help children develop their unique talents and build self-confidence.

One of the most popular initiatives was the "Art and Music Program." The school provided a wide range of artistic activities, including painting, sculpture, music, and drama. Students were encouraged to explore different forms of creative expression and find their passions. One memorable story was of a young boy named Ethan, who discovered his love for music through the school's violin lessons. With the support of his teachers, he joined the school orchestra and later won a scholarship to a prestigious music academy.

Another inspiring story was of a group of students who collaborated on a mural project. They worked together to design and paint a large mural on the school's playground wall, depicting the values of Bellwood Academy. The mural became a symbol of the school's commitment to creativity and community, and the students took great pride in their work.

The school also organized regular "Talent Shows," where students could showcase their artistic talents. These events were a celebration of creativity and provided a platform for students to share their gifts with the school community. One year, a shy girl named Lily surprised everyone with her incredible dance performance. Her talent and confidence shone through, earning her a standing ovation from her peers and teachers. The talent shows became a highlight of the school year, fostering a sense of pride and community.

Bellwood Academy also encouraged creative writing as a form of self-expression. The school organized regular "Writing Workshops," where students could explore different genres and styles of writing. One memorable story was of a student named Max, who discovered his love for poetry through these workshops. His heartfelt poems about nature and friendship were published in the school's literary magazine, inspiring other students to find their voices through writing.

In addition to visual and performing arts, the school promoted creativity in problem-solving and innovation. The "Inventors' Club" was a popular after-school activity where students could brainstorm and develop their own inventions. One year, a group of students designed a solar-powered water purifier, which won a national innovation award. Their invention not only showcased their creativity but also addressed a pressing environmental issue.

In conclusion, creative expression at Bellwood Academy allowed students to explore their talents and build self-confidence. Through art, music, writing, and innovative projects, the school created a nurturing environment where children could express themselves and develop their unique abilities.

11

Chapter 11: Global Awareness

Bellwood Academy believed in the importance of teaching children about the world beyond their immediate surroundings. The school's global awareness program aimed to broaden students' perspectives and foster a sense of empathy and responsibility as global citizens.

One of the key initiatives was the "Cultural Exchange Program." The school partnered with schools from different countries, allowing students to learn about different cultures and traditions. One memorable exchange was with a school in Japan. Bellwood students learned about Japanese customs, language, and arts, while their Japanese counterparts learned about life in Bellwood. The exchange culminated in a virtual celebration, where students from both schools shared their experiences and performed cultural presentations.

Another important aspect of global awareness was environmental education. The school's "Green Ambassadors" program encouraged students to take action on environmental issues. One inspiring story was of a group of students who organized a community-wide clean-up day. They collaborated with local organizations to clean up a nearby river, raising awareness about water pollution and conservation. Their efforts earned them recognition from the local government and inspired other schools to start similar initiatives.

To further promote global awareness, Bellwood Academy incorporated current events and global issues into the curriculum. Students engaged in discussions and debates about topics such as climate change, human rights, and global health. These activities helped students develop critical thinking skills and a deeper understanding of the interconnectedness of the world.

The school also organized "Global Citizenship Week," a week-long event dedicated to celebrating diversity and promoting global awareness. The week included guest speakers, workshops, and cultural performances. One year, the school invited Dr. Amina, a humanitarian worker, to share her experiences working in refugee camps. Her stories of resilience and compassion left a lasting impact on the students, inspiring them to get involved in humanitarian efforts.

In conclusion, global awareness at Bellwood Academy broadened students' perspectives and fostered a sense of empathy and responsibility. Through cultural exchanges, environmental education, current events, and global citizenship initiatives, the school prepared students to be informed and compassionate global citizens.

12

Chapter 12: The Role of Technology

In the digital age, Bellwood Academy recognized the importance of integrating technology into education. The school's approach to technology was not just about using gadgets and software but about leveraging technology to enhance learning and creativity.

One of the most impactful initiatives was the "Digital Learning Lab." This state-of-the-art facility was equipped with computers, tablets, and interactive whiteboards, providing students with access to a wide range of digital tools and resources. The lab offered courses in coding, digital art, and multimedia production, allowing students to explore their interests in technology. One memorable story was of a student named Mia, who created an animated short film in the lab. Her film won a regional award, showcasing her talent and creativity.

The school also introduced a "Tech for Good" program, encouraging students to use technology to solve real-world problems. One inspiring story was of a group of students who developed an app to help elderly community members access local services and support. The app was a huge success and received recognition from the local government. The project taught the students valuable lessons in empathy, problem-solving, and the positive impact of technology.

To ensure responsible use of technology, Bellwood Academy incorporated digital citizenship education into the curriculum. Students learned about online safety, digital etiquette, and the ethical use of technology. One important lesson was about the impact of social media on mental health. The school invited a psychologist to talk about the potential risks and benefits of social media, helping students navigate the digital world responsibly.

In addition to classroom learning, the school used technology to enhance communication and collaboration. The school's online platform allowed students, teachers, and parents to stay connected and engaged. Students could access assignments, submit projects, and collaborate with peers online. Teachers used the platform to provide personalized feedback and support, ensuring that each student received the attention they needed.

In conclusion, the role of technology at Bellwood Academy was to enhance learning and creativity. Through the Digital Learning Lab, the Tech for Good program, digital citizenship education, and online collaboration, the school prepared students to navigate the digital age with confidence and responsibility.

13

Chapter 13: Parental Involvement

Parental involvement was a cornerstone of Bellwood Academy's success. The school believed that collaboration between parents and teachers was essential for creating a supportive and nurturing environment for children.

One of the key initiatives was the "Parent Partnership Program." This program encouraged parents to actively participate in their children's education. Parents were invited to volunteer in the classroom, attend workshops, and join the school's advisory council. One memorable story was of Mr. and Mrs. Brown, who volunteered to teach a cooking class as part of the school's entrepreneurship curriculum. Their class became a hit, and students learned valuable lessons in teamwork, creativity, and business management.

Another important aspect of parental involvement was the school's "Family Learning Nights." These events provided opportunities for families to engage in fun and educational activities together. One year, the school organized a science fair, where students and their families conducted experiments and showcased their findings. The event fostered a sense of community and excitement for learning.

The school also provided resources and support for parents to help them navigate their children's educational journey. The "Parent Resource Center" offered workshops on topics such as positive discipline, supporting learning at home, and managing screen time. The center also provided a space for parents to connect with each other and share experiences.

To ensure effective communication, Bellwood Academy used a variety of tools to keep parents informed and engaged. The school's online platform allowed parents to access important information, such as school announcements, calendars, and student progress reports. Teachers also held regular parent-teacher conferences to discuss students' achievements and areas for growth.

In conclusion, parental involvement at Bellwood Academy created a collaborative and supportive environment for students. Through the Parent Partnership Program, Family Learning Nights, the Parent Resource Center, and effective communication, the school built strong partnerships with families, enhancing the overall educational experience.

14

Chapter 14: Celebrating Diversity

Bellwood Academy celebrated diversity and inclusivity as essential elements of its holistic education model. The school believed that embracing differences and promoting understanding would create a more compassionate and equitable community.

One of the key initiatives was the "Diversity and Inclusion Committee." This committee, composed of students, teachers, and parents, organized events and activities that celebrated the diverse backgrounds and cultures within the school community. One memorable event was the "International Food Festival," where families brought dishes from their cultural heritage to share with others. The festival was a joyous celebration of flavors, stories, and traditions, fostering a sense of unity and appreciation for diversity.

Another important aspect of celebrating diversity was the school's "Inclusive Curriculum." The curriculum included diverse perspectives and voices, ensuring that all students felt represented and valued. One inspiring story was of a literature class that studied books by authors from different cultural backgrounds. The students engaged in meaningful discussions about identity, history, and social justice, broadening their understanding of the world.

Bellwood Academy also promoted inclusivity through its "Peer Mentorship Program." This program paired older students with younger peers, providing guidance and support. One heartwarming story was of a student named Carlos, who struggled with feeling isolated after moving to Bellwood from another country. His peer mentor, Sarah, helped him navigate the new environment and build friendships. The program created a sense of belonging and community for all students.

To further promote inclusivity, the school organized "Diversity Workshops" for students and staff. These workshops covered topics such as cultural competency, anti-bullying, and allyship. One memorable workshop was led by Ms. Lee, a diversity educator, who facilitated activities and discussions that challenged stereotypes and encouraged empathy. The workshops empowered students and staff to be advocates for diversity and inclusion.

In conclusion, celebrating diversity at Bellwood Academy created a more compassionate and equitable community. Through the Diversity and Inclusion Committee, inclusive curriculum, peer mentorship program, and diversity workshops, the school fostered an environment where all students felt valued and respected.

15

Chapter 15: Looking to the Future

As Bellwood Academy continued to thrive, the school's vision for the future remained focused on holistic education. The school aimed to build on its successes and continue to innovate, ensuring that students were well-prepared for the challenges and opportunities of the 21st century.

One of the key goals was to expand the school's reach and impact. Bellwood Academy planned to share its holistic education model with other schools and communities, providing resources and support for implementation. The school's leaders envisioned a network of schools working together to promote spirituality, ethics, and entrepreneurship in childhood education.

The school also aimed to further integrate technology into the curriculum, exploring new ways to enhance learning and creativity. Plans included the development of virtual classrooms, online learning platforms, and digital collaboration tools. These advancements would provide students with access to a world full of learning opportunities. Bellwood Academy envisioned a future where students could connect with experts and peers from around the globe, fostering a more collaborative and interconnected learning environment.

Another important goal was to deepen the school's commitment to sustainability and social responsibility. The school planned to expand its environmental programs, such as the Community Garden Initiative and the Green Ambassadors program, to involve more students and community members. Bellwood Academy also aimed to introduce new projects focused on social justice, encouraging students to become advocates for positive change in their communities and beyond.

The school's leadership recognized the importance of continuous improvement and innovation. They committed to regular evaluations of the curriculum and teaching methods, seeking feedback from students, parents, and teachers. By staying responsive to the needs and interests of the school community, Bellwood Academy aimed to maintain its position as a leader in holistic education.

As the school looked to the future, it remained grounded in its core values of spirituality, ethics, and entrepreneurship. These principles would continue to guide the school's mission and vision, ensuring that Bellwood Academy remained a place where children could grow into compassionate, resilient, and innovative individuals.

In conclusion, the future of Bellwood Academy was bright and full of promise. By expanding its reach, integrating technology, deepening its commitment to sustainability and social responsibility, and continuously innovating, the school aimed to provide a holistic education that would empower students to thrive in an ever-changing world. The journey of Bellwood Academy was a testament to the power of holistic education, and its story would inspire generations to come.

Heavenly Ventures: Integrating Spirituality, Ethics, and Entrepreneurship in Childhood Education

In the quaint town of Bellwood, an innovative school emerges with a groundbreaking approach to childhood education. **Heavenly Ventures** explores the heartwarming and inspiring journey of Bellwood Academy, where the traditional curriculum is beautifully intertwined with spirituality, ethics, and entrepreneurship.

Join the vibrant community of Bellwood as they embark on this transformative journey, led by passionate educators and supported by dedicated parents and local leaders. Discover the power of mindfulness, the importance of ethical decision-making, and the excitement of entrepreneurial projects that empower young minds.

Through engaging stories and real-life examples, the book highlights the impact of holistic education on children's lives. From the shy girl who found her confidence through a baking project to the boy who discovered inner peace through mindfulness, each chapter unveils the magic of an education that nurtures both the heart and mind.

Heavenly Ventures is a celebration of creativity, resilience, and community, and a testament to the potential of integrating spirituality, ethics, and entrepreneurship into childhood education. This book is a must-read for educators, parents, and anyone passionate about fostering a holistic and meaningful educational experience for the next generation.

www.ingramcontent.com/pod-product-compliance
Lightning Source LLC
LaVergne TN
LVHW020501080526
838202LV00057B/6090